# CHAMPION BLOKES 'SHED' THEIR SHAME!

## IAN 'WATTO' WATSON

A book by Watto Books

© Ian Watson 2015

Apart from any fair dealing for the purposes of private study, research, criticism or review as permitted under the Copyright Act, no part of this book may be reproduced by any process without the written permission of the publishers.

Names and details have been changed to protect privacy.

Watto Books, PO Box 241, Woody Pt QLD 4019, Australia

wattobooks.com

ISBN: 978-0-9873788-1-1

'The Prison of Male Shame' © Frank Doolan and used by permission.

Scripture quotations labelled NIV are taken from the HOLY BIBLE, NEW INTERNATIONAL VERSION® NIV®. Copyright © 1973, 1978, 1984 by Biblica, Inc.™. Used by permission of Biblica, Inc. ™. All rights reserved worldwide. "NIV" and "NEW INTERNATIONAL VERSION" are trademarks registered in the United States Patent and Trademark office by Biblica, Inc.™.

Scripture quotations marked AMP are taken from the Amplified Bible, Copyright © 1954, 1958, 1962, 1964, 1965, 1987 by The Lockman Foundation. Used by permission.

Scripture quotations marked The Message are taken from *The Message*. Copyright © 1993, 1994, 1995, 1996, 2000, 2001, 2002. Used by permission of NavPress Publishing Group.

Scripture quotations marked ESV are taken from The Holy Bible, English Standard Version® (ESV®) Copyright © 2001 by Crossway, a publishing ministry of Good News Publishers. All rights reserved. ESV Text Edition: 2007

Cover signwriting Chad Polinski, Eternal Signs
eternalsigns.com.au

Cover photography © Peter Jendra and used by permission.

Editing, cover layout and internal illustrations
Belinda Pollard, Small Blue Dog Publishing
www.smallbluedog.com

# Reactions to *Champion Blokes 'Shed' Their Shame!*

**In-your-face honesty with real life facts and spiritual wisdom that can help you find healing in areas you didn't even know healing could be found.** Watto's done it again! Fabulous! And the personal stories are gems.
Dr Fred Gollasch, Teacher, Educator, Mentor and Co-founder of Better Blokes

As I read *Champion Blokes 'Shed' Their Shame* I am deeply moved in a good way realising where I could be had I not been surrounded by men like Ian with the courage to get fair dinkum and take a risk to tell me what I needed to hear over what people thought I wanted to hear. I am blessed and now able to pass it on as I go to help others stuck in shame. **This book has the honesty to heal many hearts as they begin to seek the hope and future God has planned.**
Wayne Neibling, Beenleigh Shed

**This book contains the blueprint to heal your heart, and tells how to 'Get Rid of Shame'.** All you have to do is get to know the Big Fella upstairs, follow the guidelines, and you'll be healed!

It's full of real-deal stories of how blokes have Shed their shame.
Peter Jendra, Retired Professional Photographer and Secondary Teacher

There is darkness and delight within this book. Darkness to show us all the reality of what life has put us through and delight to show us what life can be like if we recognise and deal with the things that hold us back. **Bless you Watto for realising your shame and putting it into terms that we can all relate to and grow from**. This book will help many, many men.
Paul Smith, Business Owner, Career Management Professionals

Ian's at it again – and thank God for that! Men need to read this book as men are bogged down in the quagmire of shame. Ian's writing style and pearls of wisdom are a rope to help any bloke wanting to get out of the shite, or **as Ian has put it, 'Shed it! Shed it! Shed it! Speak it out – get it? And be healed and free**.'
Michael Knight, Peer Power

Grief in regard to anxiety, depression, or stress – all blokes will suffer from this in one form or another. Whether you've caused someone shame or been shamed, *Champion Blokes 'Shed' Their Shame!* **will help you understand where the shame comes from, address it, and find forgiveness**. The forgiveness Watto describes is that genuine freeing of the head and heart that can only come through faith in the Big Fella upstairs. Do yourselves a favour. Pick up Watto's new little gem, and let the healing begin once again.
Tim Nagel, Airline Pilot

# Shed Happens

Thirteen years ago I helped kick off Shed Nights for blokes – not the Sheds where men work with their hands but a different type of Shed.

We start with a ripper burger in a safe non-judgemental place where men can hear real-deep gut issues – good, bad, happy or sad – through two or three blokes being interviewed up front.

No-one is allowed to preach, but only to tell their own story. You can argue with a bloke's politics or religion or footy team – but you can't argue with his story.

Shed Happens as blokes encourage each other as they do the journey of life together. They are more than happy to tell it as it is from the heart, so that others can be helped. Shed is a place where blokes are champions for who they are – not for what they are or what they have.

The original Shed Night is held on the first Monday of each month at my truckyard at Murrumba Downs, Queensland. Up to 200 blokes from all walks of life enjoy being together.

**I go to many different places in Australia helping blokes get their Sheds happening. Find the one closest to you on the shednight.com website.**

Shed blokes have played a big part in this book, and asked for nothing in return. The typical Aussie bloke doesn't need notoriety, fanfare, a fancy dress ball outfit or bells and whistles. When he's got his new heart, he just keeps putting up and putting forward at a hundred miles an hour for the benefit of others.

So that's why my book contains references to Shed and the freedom that blokes experience in their emotions, heads, souls and spirits, through being in a safe place to spill their guts and become the real deal.

Shed is the place for blokes to 'shed' their shame!

Hope you enjoy my book!

*See You In The Shed*

*Whitto*

# Foreword by Paul 'Morro' Morrison

In February 2009 I was invited to lead the singing at a blokes conference in Kalamunda, WA. There was a potato farmer from South Africa called Angus Buchan speaking all weekend and God had used him and his simple faith to influence men across South Africa and now Australia.

On the Saturday morning I was finishing sound check and I was wearing a Shed Happens T-shirt that a friend in Queensland had sent me. She had met this bloke at an Easter Festival and reckoned I would get on with him. Sitting in the front row was this robust looking bloke who yelled at me as I stepped off the stage, 'Hey mate, where did you get that t-shirt?' Not wanting to back down from this outspoken fella I said, 'OK. First you tell me where you got yours?'

He said, 'Champ, they are MY t-shirts!.'

That bloke was Watto and we have been close friends ever since.

That same morning, Angus challenged us all to have a vision for something bigger than ourselves. When Watto and I spoke over morning tea it was like that fire burning in our spirit was welding us together with a passion to see healing in the hearts of Aussie men.

Watto didn't sit around waiting for something to happen, he set to work on a book: *Every Bloke's a Champion... Even You!*

Because of that book Ian 'Watto' Watson has rapidly become a spiritual Dad to an army of Aussie blokes who are craving authenticity and someone who is fair dinkum about matters of the heart.

I have had the privilege to sit with Watto and witness blokes around this country stumbling through tears and laughing their way to healing as they are shedding the pain and hurt from their hearts – and their stories are inspiring!

In this book, Watto takes those stories and goes for the guts of his passion – seeing men free from the rubbish and lies that have held them back from becoming the real-deal blokes they were created to be.

*Champion Blokes 'Shed' Their Shame!* is written again in the straight-talking Aussie lingo that us fellas can appreciate, allowing healing and awakening in the hearts and lives of many champion men.

My prayer for this book is that one of those champions is you!

Paul 'Morro' Morrison
West Coast Eagles Chaplain, 98five Sonshine FM Breakfast

## Foreword by Phil Smith

I served alongside decorated officers and men, but a truck-driving instructor showed me courage.

I have interviewed national and world leaders, but a former public servant taught me leadership.

Few pastors or counsellors have ever shared Grace and Trust, as this husband, father and grandfather does.

No teacher ever gave me a love of 'story' – others' and my own – like this footy playing, bear-hugging, big-hearted giant of encouragement.

Ian Watson has the courage to trust other men with his own story, leads us to face and tell our own stories and, in that, points us to Grace that can transform our lives.

Mentor is a word worn thin by overuse, in a day when the the self-help industry sells men clichés, and our leaders live and die by one-liners. For the record, in the ancient world Mentor was the gentle man King Ulysses trusted to care for his son, while Ulysses went to battle in the Trojan Wars.

In the courage, wisdom and honesty on every page of this book, you will find a mentor – one you can trust during the battles that come your way.

This is a good book. Watto is a Good Bloke.

Phil Smith
Formerly ABC Radio 'Weekends with Phil'

# Foreword by Noel 'Gags' Gallagher

I am and have been involved in men's ministry for the past thirty years.

This book, in its raw and truthful tellings, opens up the hearts of Australian men to become successful men, husbands, fathers, grandfathers and Aussie citizens.

Watto has been able to capture men's failings and struggles and eventual triumphs over adversities through Faith, Hope, Love and Mercy that 'trumphs exaltantly over judgment'.

Thank you Watto for being my Mate, and for your dedication and commitment to pioneering Shed Happens for men throughout Australia. And for the two books you have published so far.

Noel 'Gags' Gallagher
Former International Rugby League Player
Player for Queensland, Australia and Cronulla Sharks during the 1960s
Recipient of Australian Sports Medal 2000 for Australian Sporting Achievement
Recipient of Centenary Medal 2001 for Services to Prisoners
Pastor and Chaplain to two men's prisons for 9 years
Founder of BADBOYSDOWNUNDER. Cares for released inmates and their families
Co-Founder/Organiser of Bribie Island Shed Happens For Men
Husband to Linda
Father to 3 sons
Grandfather to 12 grandchildren
Great Grandfather to 3 great-grandchildren (and growing!)

# Thanks!

To my champion wife Margaret for typing my book just the way it came out of my heart. She is an amazing lady.

To our three champion sons, Haydn, Brendan and Luke – for bringing joy into our lives.

To my champion editor Belinda Pollard who had to think like Watto again.

To all the champions in my life and in my Shed, who helped make this book happen.

To the Champion of champions for breathing life into me.

# 1. Watto's discovery

Hey fellas, since I wrote *Every Bloke's a Champion – Even You!* **I've got some big news for you.** I've spent the last couple of years finding out what the word 'shame' means and I've discovered how it has affected me in my life without me ever realising.

**We don't generally speak much about our shame because it's just too painful to do so.** But I've sorted out mine at last, and that's made me want to help you smash your shame too.

When I first got the message about shame, I could see so many people who have been smashed by it. I've seen so many men try so hard to get out of pain.

**I wanted to write this book in everyday language so that men could have hope to be free.**

> So much of the stuff that holds them back
>     is shame –
>         sexual shame,
>         or failure shame,
>         or being told they're idiots.

**I know that with encouragement men can turn around overnight.** I've seen so many good men come out of the pits and go on and help other men. So that's my passion to write this book.

## How it started

I can't recall ever talking about the word 'shame'. I didn't know what it really meant other than there's a dark problem.

Growing up I'd heard it said many times, 'Ian, you should be ashamed of yourself' for saying or doing something. Did you ever cop that? You know what I mean? Did anyone ever say, 'Shame on you!' People often use the word as a one-word answer with an exclamation mark: 'Shame!'

One morning, my wife Margaret heard a **champion Shed mate Phil Smith** on the radio talking about books that had influenced him. One was *Bo's Café*, a novel about a bloke facing some battles and becoming the 'real deal'.

Soon afterwards, I was on a road trip with Phil and 50 other blokes to Mundubbera to help with a flood clean up. I told Phil that Margaret enjoyed his interview.

Phil just happened to have the audio book of ***Bo's Café*** in the player of his u-beaut ute! He grabbed it and said, 'Take it and have a listen.' Man, was it for me!

Later, Margaret and I had the opportunity to go to a seminar on shame. The book and the seminar woke me up about the word shame – yes, shame.

> If it turns inwards
> you become scarred,
> all the time thinking that
> you're so bad
> and that it's your fault.
> That's how I got to believe the lie about myself.

Looking back now I know that **if my Dad had known what was going on with me, I wouldn't have been the one who needed to worry about my safety.** My abuser would have been the one who needed to be scared of my Dad.

Although my shame happened over 50 years ago and I thought I'd sorted everything out, it was so deeply hidden that I'd learned a decoy strategy. I would go after sympathy again and again for poor young 15-year-old Ian finding his mother dead on the floor and then having his 17-year-old sister collapse and die.

What a sad heart of grief. But it was a diversion. **See how easy it is to go straight back to the cover-up instead of breaking the real lie** of sexual interference and bringing it into the open for healing?

That's a natural, to drop back into what we know best. But it may not be the best place, because we're in a deep hole.

Champions, if there's something I have written that has struck a chord with you, don't do a runner, just hang on – **you can come out of this with a truckload of Gold.**

I can tell you from my own life how shame can creep up and get at us. I can also tell you what I've found out about how to kick it forever and be free in a new way – total freedom. So let's get cracking because **when a man hears it straight from the heart of another man, he 'gets' it and can learn from it!**

**There's a book that I can count on, the Bible – a proven bestseller. Give it a read – you might be surprised by how good it is, like I was! It's so practical that I call it the *Work Manual for the Champion Life*.**

---

**Here's one little gem:**

As iron sharpens iron, so one man sharpens another. (Proverbs 27:17 NIV)

---

## Everyone has big and little shames

**There's no shame in shame.**

It has a go at every man, woman and child at some time in our lives. It's been around since Adam played fullback for Jerusalem.

If you don't think this is for you at the moment, **HANG ON TO IT. IT'S A KEEPER!** I guarantee that either you or someone close to you will appreciate it somewhere or sometime in life.

Shame can be caused by things other people have done to us, or by things we have done ourselves.

**Shame has been around since Adam played fullback for Jerusalem**

They can be big shames. For example, you might have been unfaithful in your marriage and gone to a prostitute or had a one-night stand – and ended up with a sexually transmitted disease. And then you had to face the reality – you couldn't hide. You had the shame of admitting: this is what I've done wrong. For a man it's easier to just shut down and hide.

They can be little and subtle shames.

> **Watch out for the little ones,**
> **because they can be just as destroying**
> **as the big 'uns.**
> **Things like**
> **being called names,**
> **and told you're an idiot,**
> **you're hopeless,**
> **you're a d—head.**

Depending on the personality of the person, when you're young you can be smitten into nothingness. Other people might toughen up and say it doesn't matter. But because **we're all different and not sausages out of a sausage factory**, we need to be able to help each person on the journey, where they're at.

There are many things in life that can pin us down for a while but don't have deeply damaging effects.

As a primary school boy I had times where I was ashamed that I went to the small Boondall School that had only 1 class per grade when Sandgate was the big school where they had 5 classes in each year. They won all the interschool comps and we were scared to play them 'cause we'd get the cr*p beaten out of us. **These little shame things left memories but not scars.**

As you read on, little things that are stuck deep down in you will emerge. And you'll think, 'That was nothing… but it clung on!'

> that triggered the shame
> and you finally give up and let go.
>
> Grace shows up.
>
> This is the healing stuff from the Big Fella,
> into your heart and soul –
> and that's what happened for me.

We'll talk about grace a little further down the track. **Grace is more than a girl's name!**

I grew up a little fearful of my good old Dad. I was always feeling a bit guilty and scared, and that's probably why at times I was a bit scared of my Dad. I know it was silly now, 'cause that's not how it was with him as I became a man.

But as a kid I thought he was just a big, serious and sometimes grumpy boss – all rules and no fun. So deep down that's how I related to God. I got sidetracked.

I just wish I'd learned how to love and trust Dad, because when I called out to God I needed to let him teach me how to trust him. It wasn't easy for me 'cause I had too many negative people and different opinions creating confusion in my mind, and that bred distrust.

> I now tell shame out aloud:
> 'Get out of my head and my heart.
> You are the loser.

> You have no hold on any part of me ever again.'
> And I let it go through to the Keeper.
>
> I am Watto.
>
> I choose Freedom
> and choose to be the real-deal me.
> That's what makes me a champion.

Just letting you know that the person who shamed me passed on a few years ago and my heart and mind are free. Everyone's situation is different, but my journey to freedom never involved any financial compensation.

**I certainly don't want to inflict any shame on anyone connected with that person 'cause my wish for all people is for them to know that they are OK and they have a hope and a future.**

I'm not saying it's wrong to get a payout if you were abused – I don't even want to go into that subject. But I want to be very clear that if you think a financial payout will help you get free of your shame, I don't think it will get to the bottom of it. You have to get down into the core of who you are to be free of the shame.

**I very clearly know that it was the good and great men and women who invested into my life – you could call them my 'village' – who loved me and helped me expose**

**my pain and shame.** Because of them, I didn't even need to go to a professional counsellor on shame.

But again, had I not had the love and nurture of community, of my 'village', and the ability to be loved and expose my shame in a safe, non-judgemental place, I wouldn't be where I am today. Don't be afraid to seek out a counsellor if needed.

## Rocks around the heart

This showed me why I needed to do the 'heart journey' I wrote about in Chapter 12 of my book *Every Bloke's a Champion – Even You!* **I had to get rid of all the rocks around my heart so that I could be more the real-deal champion I was created to be.** Then I was ready to tackle this shame thing that eats down into the core of man and woman just like cancer.

---

**A little gem from the *Work Manual for the Champion Life***

A new heart will I give you and a new spirit
will I put within you, and I will take away the
stony heart out of your flesh and give you
a heart of flesh. (Ezekiel 36:26 Amp)

---

I recognised my 'shame moment' and I spoke it out to the Big Fella. Bit-by-bit, as it showed up. **He knows every bit of my new and old heart and I accepted his true freedom.** God then smashed my shame at the cross. Jesus had the absolute shame of being naked on a cross. He copped a lot of shame to give us freedom.

## Shame smashes a bloke

**Can you see now why I played my footy so mean and dirty?** To get rid of some shame pain through deep simmering anger.

**I overdid the aggressive bit on those full-forwards**, and I never really knew why. Thanks to all you great opponents for helping me with my 'anger management'! I wish I could have said sorry to those full-forwards that I bashed, but at least the umpires gave them plenty of free kicks anyway.

I also remember feeling some relief by overpowering different people with **verbal bullying, thinking I was just being funny**. I pulled them into my hidden pain of shame. Not nice!

How do you think my head felt towards homosexuals after what I went through as a boy? It seemed a given and a natural to be an accuser and judge.

Watching my abuser every Sunday pushing himself out the front at church as a musician like he was Mr Goody Good just fuelled my anger, and at the time I took my eyes off God. I probably blamed God for what that man did. I went into judgement of the 'system' and his lifestyle because of his shameful acts that could hide behind church and religion.

> **You get to lift your head up
> when you know you're free of shame.**

I know another bloke, a good man, who is in a bad place. He broke the law because of his gambling habit. He did his time in prison, and was rebuilding his life. Now he's gone back into shame because he stole from a family member to gamble again.

He's so shameful about it that he thinks he doesn't even deserve to live. He's got a job, so I told him straight out, 'Start paying it back.' There's freedom from shame, even if you've stuffed it up. Face what you've done, and start again.

---

**Get a load of this gem from the *Work Manual***

'You, O Lord, are a shield about me, **my glory, and the lifter of my head**.' (Psalm 3:3 ESV)

---

I hope you can hang in with me on this because **the more I speak with men throughout our beautiful country, the more crippled by shame I see we are**, or have been. Fellas, it's helping destroy those we love most. **It's time to look up and get our chins up.**

Freedom for us can mean freedom for the thousands of others we do life with. We don't have to preach to anyone or try to push them – just tell our story of freedom from shame.

# 2. The Prison of Male Shame

One of my champion mates **Riverbank Frank from Dubbo** has written a Shame Poem for you. Hope you enjoy it.

There's a prison in Australia
Where you cop all the blame
It's lonely doing life
**In the prison of 'male shame'**
Little boys in Australia
As we grow into men
We're taught to be silent to be strong
To keep the bad stuff in

When memories from your past
Are tearing you apart
It's easier to black it out
Than to listen to your heart
Talking with a mate can help
But with Australian men
If it's a painful shame
We won't go there again!

We bottle up emotion
We hold onto the hurt
**Prisoners of 'male shame'**
Always feel like dirt
So many Australian men
Live with pain they try to hide
In despair and desperation
They turn to suicide

Brothers there is another way
To cope with inner pain
Internalising grief holds you
**In the prison of 'male shame'**
A touch of self-forgiveness
Self-love and not self-hate
**And we're Australian men my brothers**
**So share your troubles with a mate**


## Frank Doolan (Riverbank)

# 3. Don't be shamed by shame

Shame has no preference – other than to take good champions and pull down their self-worth. **Shame will have you believing the lie that you're a failure, you should not have been born, that you're a mistake.** Shame can nail us right back at birth – or even earlier when in the womb. Get the idea? This can peck away at your mind.

### How shame starts

**Shame is born from our unmet or failed expectations – deep, deep down at the core of who we are.** We come to a point where we believe a lie, **it can be a big one or little ones,** and we bash ourselves on the inside with cruel judgement. We say things like:

    I can't do anything right

    I'm a bad person

    I'm a mistake

    I'm unforgiveable

    I'm a loser

I'm an idiot

I'm hopeless

I'm not good enough.

**Shame can go on to drag us into sadness, despair and depression.**

> **Sometimes,
> because we believe we're so bad,
> we can't forgive ourselves.**
>
> **We begin to think even God can't forgive us.
> We couldn't go into a church, we're so bad.**
>
> **Rubbish and rot!
> That's the absolute opposite
> of what the Big Fella has for us!**

## Shame and families

Now I want to take you to have a look back at the type of family you grew up in, and open your mind to see if you have anything that may have caused you to take on shame.

Your first thought here might be that your childhood was shame free. Take care and have a look at these few points because that can be where you began to believe a lie about yourself – just like I did. If you're not careful, to varying degrees your self-worth can be stolen from you at any time.

## The family of neglect

**Did you feel neglected?**

**Did either or both of your parents show you little or no value?**

**Did they act like you didn't exist?**

This might be how you saw and felt it as a junior burger, even if it's not necessarily how it was from your parents' point of view. My sisters didn't feel the same as me, even though we were in the same house. And when I got older I realised that the way I saw my parents wasn't right. But you can only call it as you saw it. It's your story. We see it from our own point of view, and it can cause us to take on shame.

Maybe you grew up thinking that there was something wrong with you because your parents showed no interest in what was important to you.

Were you left alone to cry and not picked up and cuddled?

I know some blokes who were sent to boarding school because their parents were very busy with their business. **Being sent away to boarding school can affect some children so that they feel neglected**, especially if they only see their parents a couple of times a year. They can believe they're 'in the way' of their parents and feel rejected and ashamed. Was it this way for you?

What if your parents went on an overseas mission and you were sent to boarding school? How did you feel about God, church and religion?

## The army barracks

Did you grow up in a family that may as well have been an Army Barracks?

**You were treated like you were a number and not a name and your self-worth was smashed into nothingness.** You were expected to act, not to think. Click your heels, salute and say 'Yes sir'.

You weren't allowed to make a mistake. Mother and/or father called all the shots like a sergeant. You became a 'yes man' and it was so rigid – with rules, rules, more rules – so you just went inward and silence became your comfort and your weapon.

## The fruit salad

**What about a family that's linked like a fruit salad where everybody was so enmeshed together that your sense of individuality was lost and taken away?**

You know, you felt like a sausage coming out of the sausage factory, or one of the baked beans in the tin. You had no identity as an individual. You had to do everything together. You weren't allowed to query anything. You didn't feel as though you could be yourself. None of your own creativity and sparkle could come out.

You might have been shamed by your family for trying to spend time away from them, or for wanting to be an individual or do something different.

## The abusive home

Or did you grow up in an abusive home?

You may have lived under **emotional** abuse and could never do anything right. You were told you were the wrong sex, you came at the wrong time or you should have been left at the hospital.

Or were you a product of rape? Your mother or father tried to have you aborted and told you later in life.

You may have lived in terror through **domestic violence** between parents or other grown-ups in the house. You had lots of anxiety and fear **from physical abuse.**

Or you didn't know that the words 'discipline' and 'respect' even existed. You were given no guidelines, made your own rules, and brought yourself up. You didn't know what counted as 'foul' language, and you wondered why your schoolteachers didn't get it that you didn't know.

Or sadly, you suffered **sexual abuse** as a child and have lived your later life feeling like an object. You may feel dirty, guilty, worthless and used, and you still feel the deep shame, deep within you.

I know a young man who suffered sexual abuse as a boy and as soon as he was able he changed his name to get away from the shame of his family name in his district. You may be struggling sexually in a current relationship as a result of early abuse. There are many sad consequences that can haunt and hinder you from having a normal healthy sex life.

## Johnno's family shame 'moment'

This is my mate Johnno's story, in his own words.

> **Shame to me was having that feeling that I was a complete failure in life.** I had no encouragement from my stepfather but was only put down. I never got a hug or a pat on the back when I did things right. Shame to me was living with my past and the guilt that had dragged me under. Then came the other and total shame when I had to admit to myself and others that I was an alcoholic.
>
> But today I realise that Jesus died on the cross for me. He took the bullet for me so I could be free of shame and sin. He defeated the devil so that I may be free."

**Johnno's moment is just one of the shame stories from a few of my Shed mates around the country that I've included in the book.** They have willingly contributed their stories to help others gain freedom. I've changed names and some details to give them some privacy, but their stories are the real deal. Should one of these stories speak to you in particular, contact the writers through me at my website, **wattobooks.com.**

# 4. Don't confuse guilt with shame

We need to be sure to clean up another possible diversion about shame. **Don't confuse guilt with shame. It's totally different.**

**Guilt** = I've done something wrong.

**Shame** = I am wrong.

> We're all going to be guilty of many things,
>     said and done,
>     big or little,
>     bad or not so bad.
> But when you get to know
>     you've made a mistake and are guilty,
>         as soon as you can,
>             admit it
>             and apologise
>             and say you are sorry.
> Ask for forgiveness where necessary
>     for the mistake you made
>     or the comment you made.
> Try to grab it by the throat straight off.

**If we can right a wrong as soon as possible and not do it again it can make us better not bitter.** We can quickly learn from it and turn it into a positive. We are better off learning from our mistakes and getting on with it.

You can be guilty of a sinful act and you don't know where to turn. You can bash your heart so hard that you further hurt the ones closest to you, 'cause you can't be free to love.

So love dies on the inside, and no-one really knows why. This doesn't need to happen.

**Forgiveness is the key and we may need lots of help, 'cause we have trouble forgiving ourselves. Light, love and patience can be the best helpers** with step-by-step forgiveness that may take time – the 'right' time, and sometimes plenty of it.

With the help of the Big Fella, it's doable.

## When we don't admit it

But if you don't admit it, **you can let it turn inwards, so be careful 'cause guilt can end up becoming shame.** Then you've gone from doing something wrong to believing you are a bad person, and that's rubbish. We all make mistakes and that's that. Apologise from your heart, change your ways, and move on – no more sorry, sorry.

This one can take a lot of courage. Sorry is more than just a word. It may need relearning to see and act differently – a big call. You may need help to change your thinking.

**Don't take past guilt into shame. It's your choice. Tell shame to ping off.** Sadness can turn into depression and can turn inwards into shame. Expose this lie at the first glimpse.

> **Shame would like to hold us in guilt
> and turn it inwards upon us.
> We can let this creep up on us
> without even knowing.**
>
> **It's like a cancer sneaking up on us
> and eating us out from the inside.**

This can happen over a long period of time. It will wear us down and hold us back, robbing us of our freedom. We can wonder why it is that we can't get moving. That's how easy it is to believe the lie that has lodged in our head. It can be like living without blue sky. When you have only the dark clouds over you it can push you toward oppression of your spirit. Dead Man Walking stuff!

So fellas, you can now see how big this becomes. There are not many nice things that happen around shame. These areas I have mentioned are just the tip of the iceberg.

**The great news is that you can kill it and get on with a full, free and open shameless life. Be encouraged.** Wow, pow!

## The media loves shame

You may notice how **the Press doesn't like apology. They want to destroy people in shame, especially leaders.** This can include coaches, TV personalities, prominent people, church leaders.

Just look at the Prime Ministers and Premiers throughout Australian governments over the past ten years. The media seems to enjoy holding them guilty on most issues. The pollies spend most of their time in office in survival mode.

**The Press don't seem to like to hear a 'sorry I've made a mistake'** from anyone. They'd rather just grind on with the shame game. Leaders can be dodging bullets more than running the country. They may come in with creativity and fresh initiatives but that can be held back with the guilt attacks.

**We'd make more progress if we encouraged more.**

> ### A gem from the *Work Manual*
> Do not withhold good from those who deserve it, when it is in your power to act. (Proverbs 3:27 NIV)

**You know, silent judgement is still judgement** – best replaced by encouragement. It would be good if we blokes

could encourage some of our media to take this up.

## Dream-takers love shame

Be aware that **there are plenty of dream-takers around who don't want to accept your apology** for a mistake. They delight in holding you guilty to the point of trying to drive you into shame. They can keep at you. This can be a sad payback to a relationship break-up.

## Mac's story

One of my Shed mates lived out another kind of shame from his childhood, and his story may be a great help to you or someone you know.

Mac started school at age 4. Most of his schoolmates were 5 or 6 so he was always the little bloke in the class. Mac always wanted to be in the back row with the big blokes for the class photo, but every year he was the one holding the Grade Board in the middle of the front row.

His Dad was middle-aged when Mac was born so at school functions his classmates used to think Mac had his grandparents there because the other children's parents were younger. The kids at school hurt Mac when they called them his grandparents.

**Mac was always the last bloke picked for a team and he couldn't fight any of his own fights because he was too scared.** He was always looking for someone to cover for him.

As a teenager he was shy and introverted and was scared of girls. He even grew his blond hair long to try to win the girls – until a carload of blokes whistled at him and thought he was a girl. So that made him grow a beard real fast. He felt a complete and utter loser.

**Mac's entire life up to 6 years ago was driven by being a very needy person who never ever felt good enough.** He had very low self-esteem.

He did something similar to what I did. You don't even know you're doing it, but can only see it when you look back on it.

> Every time I said,
> 'I found my mother dead on the floor
> when I was 15',
> everyone would say,
> 'Oh you poor little thing'
> and it instantly picks you up.
> You don't even realise
> but you can keep going back to that,
> and it keeps covering up
> what really makes you angry or sad.

I used my grief to get sympathy as a diversion, and Mac unknowingly sucked up to people who, without realising what they were doing, kept him in the belief that he was not good enough. He found plenty of people pleasers to hold him in shame by saying, 'You poor, poor fellow'. That was the only way he knew to get some attention. But by doing this he didn't associate with people who would call it as it is and tell him what he really needed to hear. He was scared of reality.

## Mac's marriage

Sadly, Mac and his wife divorced, and he spiralled to his lowest point of 'poor me' choices. During that period he showed little respect for women. Before healing he was ashamed of his behaviour in this messy part of his separation.

Mac now looks back at areas in that marriage where his 'poor me' behaviour would have put his wife under pressure because she didn't know how to help him, or herself. Neither of them knew any other way.

Mac and his wife had always been believers in God and attended church, but they had never associated the intimacy part of marriage with the spiritual. This part of their marriage failed dismally, guided by society's way which is based on lust. Sadly, no-one at church could guide them to the Big Fella's way.

## Mac's healing

Mac now sees that a healing journey needs more than good advice for him to come out from shame completely. To this day he continues on a healing journey choosing to go straight to the top, no middleman – straight to God for his healing of shame.

> ### A gem from the *Work Manual*
> Do not be afraid: you will not suffer shame. Do not fear disgrace; you will not be humiliated. You will forget the shame of your youth …. (Isaiah 54:4 NIV)

> **Mac also knows the need
> to gently love and empower his children
> who paid the price of pain
>     from the family break-up.**

He says that children suffer big time through the journey of break-up and the accompanying shame. They, too, need to be loved through to healing. Mac chooses to draw a line in the sand so his children are free and so he doesn't pass shame onto his grandchildren.

After his marriage break-up Mac was devastated. He lost all his friends and was smashed financially and emotionally. He didn't think he would ever be able to consider another chance at marriage. But now Mac and his new wife together endeavour to leave any past shame behind and not bring any into their marriage. Mac is a healed champion today and is helping others into freedom.

**Don't be ashamed by shame.**

**Go for healing.**

- **Receive love and encouragement from someone** you trust with the real you. They will not condemn you but will listen.
- Healing and freedom from shame is easier when you are in a strong community with others who love and support you. Grab any community love that's available, whether it's a few or a lot – like your close mates, your footy team, your church family.

Blokes, if you do Shed Happens you'll have that real-deal support and encouragement from blokes there. Check out **www.shednight.com** for locations.

Mac encourages all men not to make judgements about other women's body shapes or any other downgrading comments, especially in front of the woman you love. It can have a negative effect on her. She can take it to mean you are having a subtle go at her – it can be that touchy. So, no double messages of judgement fellas. Let's cut it out so the best can come out in us and our women.

## Are you like Mac?

Are you like Mac? Are you constantly defending yourself for every little problem? Do you hate fronting up to the real problem? Do you shoot the blame in someone else's direction to divert attention from yourself?

Or do you feel like that last bloke standing when the teams are selected and no-one knows where to put you? They just add you on to the tail because they have to include you.

> Can you see
> that your little pity party
> could be to cover your pain from shame?
> Maybe you're hiding behind
> overeating,
> drinking,
> gambling,
> medication,
> working,
> perfectionism
> or sucking-up-ism?
>
> Come on,
> you are now equipped to **have-a-crack**
> at wiping it out forever.
> You are OK!

### God has plans for you!

Back when I was a boy it was all about, 'Toughen up Watto. Forget about it and get on with it. Don't be a sook.' **The best was still to come from me, and the best is still to come from you, too.**

Who'd have ever thought I'd be able to write a book for blokes – and as an unknown author to have the book self-published?

I'm excited knowing that I'm OK and I'm pretty special in the eyes and heart of the Big Fella. I'm not 'unknown' to him. He has plans for me. **If he could use a donkey to talk, then he could use me to write a book.**

What could he get you to do?

> **Another little gem from the *Work Manual*:**
>
> 'For I know the plans I have for you,' declares the Lord, '**plans to prosper you and not to harm you, plans to give you hope and a future.** Then you will call upon me and come and pray to me, and I will listen to you. You will seek me and find me when you seek me with all your heart. I will be found by you,' declares the Lord. (Jeremiah 29:11-14a NIV)

# 5. What about you?

So how are you going with this Big Clanger – shame? It sure gets you thinking. Don't walk away from this battle – you can beat it! It may take more than one knockout punch – you might have to do ten rounds. But as long as you get the points at the end of the fight, you win!

If you think that you have no shame and that you're on top of your game, don't close this book **'cause this is the single biggest thing that holds men and women back from the best of their lives. It would be rare to find someone – man or woman – who has slipped under the radar and missed out on some form of shame.** The good news is that everybody can win over this and get the Gold.

My wish for you as we roll out one of the toughest subjects to tackle is for you to be able to identify any area – large or small – that has held you back and tried to make you believe you are no good or you're less than anyone else. It has stolen your self-worth and made you feel very low.

> **Mate, I want you to know that
> this journey is winnable.
> You will gain Gold
> right through to the absolute victory over shame.**

## Shame triggers

Fellas, as you get down the track a bit in life you may be hit with some of the following:

- a failed business
- a money crisis
- made to take a redundancy/forced retirement
- a big hit to your mental or physical health
- deep depression
- surviving a trauma – like a car accident or going to a war zone
- knowing you have a sexually-transmitted disease and you have to tell your wife or girlfriend
- rape – either being born as the product of it, or having been the offender
- shame when your boss belittles you in front of a customer
- shame when a family member is in prison and you try to cover it up so no-one knows
- addiction to internet porn – and you find you can't perform sexually
- shame from other addictions
- the shame of aborting your child
- being told you are a d—head all the time
- a failed ministry

- a political career wrecked by a loss at the election.

Several more champion Shed blokes wanted to tell their shame stories of healing. I'll let them tell you in their own words. See if their stories make you start thinking about anything in your own life, big or small.

## Johnno's story

❝Shame for me was when I couldn't look a person in the eye – I had my head down because of guilt and sin in my life. I was a failure, feeling helpless and all alone. My children were gone, my marriage was over. I felt totally defeated so I withdrew from society and became isolated. There was only me and my best friend the bottle left.

**People avoided me – I was in lockdown. My heart was like a rock, I was like an island, and every day was like a winter's day.**

My boss was kind to me. He helped me through my dark days, and he took me to rehab, because I had become an alcoholic. I was addicted to alcohol for decades.

I spent 18 months in rehab. It was a spiritual program and I was an atheist – what a challenge!

**I went upstairs and got to know the Big Fella on a first-name basis.** I made amends to my children and everyone I had harmed around me.

I found that the Lord had already forgiven me. He died on the cross for me – he took the bullet for me. This enabled me to forgive myself, which freed me from shame and guilt.

When I graduated from rehab, my daughter who I hadn't seen for many years came to my graduation. She stood in front of me and said these words, 'I love you and I forgive you.' The emotions were at their peak. I had been forgiven just like the Lord had forgiven me from Day 1.

My mum said to me, 'Welcome back, son.' I said, 'I've always been here.' She said, **'I lost you the day you picked up a drink.'**

It's like the Lord said, 'I've always been here, you just had to open the door and let me in.' Through shame and guilt I had shut the door on everyone, but through opening the door and allowing others in I found restoration through the Lord.

**I don't have that feeling of shame, loneliness, guilt and failure any more. The rocks around my heart have been replaced with diamonds.**

**Today my head is held high and I need not look down. There is no shame. Shame is a lie.**

Connection and encouragement are my tools that I have been given to help others. **It's hard to slide uphill if you're sitting on your bum.** In other words, it's a life of actions.

We didn't come to watch, we came to play, and be part of life – no shame! Game on!"

## Davo's story

"I grew up on a family farm. I loved farming and always said, 'One day I will own my own farm.' I enjoyed the challenge of growing crops and developing farms. Some called me a workaholic.

I was told by my grandmother that there is no such word as can't. She would say if you put your mind to it and work hard enough you can do anything, and that's how I wanted others to see me.

At 20, I found myself managing the family farm, which had a large debt. It was the 1980s and interest rates were over 20%. **When I had to let the farm be sold, I felt that I had let our family down.** I was the fourth generation to live on this farm and now it was gone. I was offered a job managing someone else's farm.

This sense of failure and shame affects the way you see yourself and the way you think others see you. Often it is not true, but when you think your identity is gone it is hard, very hard not to feel shame, and that you are a failure.

I still visit that farm every few years. There are a lot of memories there.

## Round 2 for Davo

At 40, life was going pretty good with a beautiful wife and kids. I'd worked my guts out to acquire another farm, a rundown property. It was going great and we built our dream home. I was starting to think I was just about bulletproof. I was set.

I would have called myself a good husband and father although **I didn't have much time for family and less time for God. People would say to me, 'You need to slow down, Davo, and smell the roses.'** I used to think, 'There is plenty of time to do that later and there are lots of flowers in heaven.'

Things are usually not how we think they are. Debt caught up with us when the drought bit hard. We had no income yet we still had all the expenses. Then our crops got a disease that no-one could identify. **I tried everything I could to save our dream farm. It seemed the harder I tried, the harder the doors would close in my face.**

Eventually the bank revalued the farm at less than half of what it had been valued 12 months before. I started dealing with all the thoughts of failure again. The lie that I was a failure resurfaced with thoughts of: could I have done things differently? I also had thoughts of the 'bastard bank'. My thinking took me into a spiral down to shame.

## Davo's time of losing it all

I had never had depression before and actually did not have much time for people who had 'off days'.

I call this time 'the stripping away time'. I knew I was losing it. All I had worked for was going and who I thought I was, was being stripped away by the day. What were my family and friends thinking?

These were my thoughts: 'I am a failure! How am I going to pay everyone? **How am I going to provide for my family? Everything is going to be sold and we are going to be homeless.'**

There were days when I would think everything was hopeless and life was becoming darker by the day. I was so low but I wouldn't go to a doctor. These days were hard and long and I often had trouble sleeping at night. **I didn't want to go to town where locals would see me. There were days when I couldn't even answer the phone.**

Eventually the bank said they were going to take over. We had come to the end. We had put everything into this business and it had failed. I was a failure.

There were a couple of weeks we didn't have any food. I couldn't even put food on the table for my family. **When**

**true friends helped us it was very hard to accept.** I felt I had completely failed.

I had to put off all our staff because we couldn't pay them. **This was one of the lowest days of my life.** I felt I had let them down and failed them too – believing the lie of shame.

## Davo's healing

An amazing thing happened the next day when 3 blokes turned up ready to work. I explained to them again that I couldn't pay them but they said they would keep working for me without pay. **This was probably the most humbling moment in my life and I still get emotional about this.** Once the bank took over they paid me and the 3 workers to maintain the property until the settlement date.

Because of my faith and belief in God I never lost hope even while all was being stripped away. Man, it was painful.

**I saw that my identity had been in my work and my big property and how I wanted to be seen by those around me. I came to know that it was all just Stuff.**

God has shown me and my wife and children that he always had a plan for us. Now he has restored us with another farm and we're successfully working through our previous debts. We are really grateful to God for this.

Shame is not on God's agenda for anyone. I am secure in my identity knowing who I am and Whose I am and free of this past shame.

**Society's way of seeing failure is that it's the end, but in God's kingdom it's the beginning.** No more do I believe the lie."

---

## Jim and Bill's story

Jim became a Christian as a 14-year-old boy at a Christian camp. An older Christian bloke, Bill, became his mentor at youth rallies, a fishing partner, a confessor who consistently encouraged him in his faith and took him and others to rallies and youth events and camps.

When Jim was 19 and a youth leader himself, the older man sexually molested him while he was sleeping. Jim jumped up in surprise and naturally objected. The older man was upset – so was he. Jim said he needed to go out for a run to clear his head.

When he returned, Bill was kneeling beside his bed praying. He said, **'Jim! We need to confess our sins.'**

**Jim said, 'Bill, you need to confess your sins.** I was asleep.'

Jim left immediately and did not have much to do with Bill after that. Forty-eight years later, Jim went back to a Sunday School reunion. Bill was there. **He came up to Jim, shook** hands and said, 'I would like you to forgive me for what I did all those years ago.'

Jim was moved by this courage and act of reconciliation. He said, **'Bill I have long since forgiven you and am only too aware that we are all sinner and saint.** I give back to you a gem from the Work Manual you gave me when I was 15 and came to you for help when I had sinned: "The Lord makes firm the steps of the one who delights in him; **though he may stumble, he will not fall, for the Lord upholds him with his hand.**" (Psalm 37:23–24 NIV).'

They hugged one another. Bill said, smiling, 'This has been one of the high moments of my spiritual life.' Later they talked about being able to see themselves through God's eyes. Bill talked about his marriage, his kids and dealing with his sexual problems – how he now works with a men's group in the local town.

Jim says this was one of the high moments of his spiritual life too – utterly liberating for both men. Both are living with a broader, deeper, more forgiving and accepting perspective. **Jim's wife says: 'History has a soft focus – God can use lots of time to bring about his purposes.'**

## PJ's story

❝I'm finding that I can't write about shame – not because it wasn't a huge reality in my past that dictated the direction of the first 43 years of my life, not because it wasn't the evil, insatiable, all-consuming 'monster' that permanently lived in my head and ruled the precinct unchallenged – **but because now I'm not ashamed.**

I remember the day the final crushing blow that my marriage was over was delivered. I was standing in front of a truck and my knees went from under me. As I grovelled in the gravel trying unsuccessfully to stand I ended up further under the truck. My only memory of focus was the sump of the engine. The 'monster' of shame was rap dancing. He'd won – mission accomplished – to kill, steal and destroy.

**Business gone. Purpose gone. Possessions gone. Identity gone. Home gone.** All I had to do now was suicide, and his book could be closed and filed. At the time, that certainly seemed like my best option to escape the pain.

I had the chain set up in the shed and the stepladder beside it. I sat there at times when the pain was completely unbearable with the chain firmly around my neck and rocking the ladder defiant in the fact that the only thing I possessed was the right to my own death.

There was only one counteracting thought at that time and that was the question of eternity. **If I died in that state of turmoil and pain would I ever actually escape it?**

## PJ's turning point

A couple of months later, I was walking aimlessly up the street of a big country town. I bumped into an acquaintance who asked me to go to church with her. I grew up in a Christian home but really hated going to church. But that Sunday I had nowhere to go and absolutely nothing left to lose, so I went.

**I regard the people in that congregation who took me in in my darkest hour as angels that worked like the clowns at a rodeo – they distracted the 'monster' long enough for me to escape certain death.**

There was no miracle instant transformation that day but it was certainly a turning point and the beginning of the end for the monster. God spoke very directly to me through the pastor of that church. Week after week his teachings of forgiveness and healing connected with me like a bull's-eye shot.

## PJ's healing

Later that year I was offered a job harvesting grain. My boss gave me a worn-out bomb of a machine and 1000 hectares of wheat to harvest by myself. As much as it frustrated me, it was the beginning of me regaining my self-worth and purpose.

We fought the battle for this farm and although it was ultimately lost to the bank, there were numerous victories for God. **It was a very poor result for the 'monster' who threw every available resource at my boss's faith but** never once cracked it. Faith in God was the foundation that we held firm to.

I was at a bloke's breakfast a year after my marriage break-up, and nobody there knew me. A visiting prophet pointed to me and said, **'You have lost everything and God is going to restore your business.'**

It was a lot of work, but two years later, I got an opportunity and my business turned around. I put my last $200 into a newspaper advert, and 18 months later my business was a huge success.

**I'm not ashamed of the lost farms, the droughts, the debts, the divorce, the ultimate of failure rubbed in my face. I don't blame myself or anyone else for the cacky parts of the journey anymore or wonder at what point in history it went wrong for me because that's what it is – history.**

**Its lessons are never forgotten, but history lives in the archives, safely stored but not in the way of the future.**

The grief is done, the anger is gone, the bitterness replaced by sweet restoration of family relationships and successful business. I recently spent time with my ex-wife and the kids. Real friendships have evolved. The future is eagerly anticipated. Sure there are struggles, but they are things to deal with, not food for the 'monster'. The tally book only counts what I have got – and that's always enough.

So let's always acknowledge the battle but make the biggest noise in claiming the victory over shame!
Thank you Jesus for dying on the cross to set me free."

---

## Many different 'moments' of shame

Everyone has a different shame story. Yours might be like one of these stories, or it might be completely different.

Keep in mind that 'those in the know' quote that one in 3 girls and one in 7 boys are sexually interfered with in their early days. If you're in these stats with me – keep your radar up to see if your past goes back to something similar and to things you used to cover it.

**Shame from body shape and looks is interesting for me as I get older – I can only do the 'after' ads** to the body beautiful these days. Ha ha! But then the counter to any shame is to remember your body is more than just the outside. Thank God for that, and know that it's what's on the inside that counts most.

We can develop our sense of humour and our creativity and show more care and love for others. **You know, when you look on the inside of another person, you'll see that they're no bigger or better than you.** We're all in the game of life together – just with different battles.

# 6. Sorting out shame

Let's continue to dig around to sort through the rubble and rubbish and slag of the past, or what might be going on right now in your life of shattered dreams. I know that you can look forward to sorting it out.

> If the stories you've read here
> remind you of any part of you,
>     don't stress.
> You'll be able to look at the bigger picture
>     of body, mind and spirit
> and you'll be able to make your own call.
> No-one is going to push you into
>     believing in the Big Fella,
> but I want to make sure
> you don't get pushed away from
>     the spiritual part of who you are.
> Got it?
> You'll be able to consider all the facts
>     and make your choice.

The Big Fella has finally got through and guided my learning journey. He wiped my shame away forever and gave me the practical part of this to pass on in my book to you.

## Watto's way to pray about this

Dear God,
You give me gems in your *Work Manual*. **It says that if I trust you, I will never be put to shame.** Please teach me to trust you so I can come through with no shame.

Fellas, no worries if you want to pray with your eyes open. It's OK, I do it all the time. I've had plenty of talks to him while I was alone driving my truck and I sure wasn't able to close my eyes while driving. **If you've never prayed before it's OK with God to keep your eyes open and do it just like you're talking to another person.**

He knows your heart and your motives. He blew your first breath into you. Just use your everyday lingo. **Don't try to make up some super-spiro stuff. He doesn't need that.**

Don't be shy of the spiritual part of who you are. After 25 years of one-on-one with blokes learning to drive a truck, I have learned that we men are generally shy.

> We're very, very shy
>     when it comes to our spiritual part
> and no-one can tell me why.
> But deep down we are spiritual,
>     when we're in a safe, non-judgemental place.

**The world's view of us is body, mind and... who knows?** So you see gyms in most shopping centres and we're spending plenty on organic food with an expectation for healthier bodies. The world has plenty of seminars and how-to's for your mind and for making a squillion.

**But the world we live in can't seem to work out the spirit part.** It's too hard to work out the church politics stuff and the 'God is our Father' part. And we usually get the wrong message about Jesus and the Spirit.

I'm not beating around the bush here. In every area that I kept away from the spiritual me I have been the loser – in footy, trotting horses, my relationship with Margaret and my business. You get what I mean? This is big stuff. Think about it.

Fellas, champions, **I hope that my take on all this can give all men the big picture of the real-deal bloke – body, mind and spirit – so you can make your own choice for the Gold. Don't complicate it. Just give it a whirl.**

## Mark's story

❝I grew up with two sisters. I was a very anxious, lonely and shy boy and it was easy for me to keep to myself and shut down. I mainly spent time with my mother and sisters because my Dad worked away. When he did have contact with me it was at the end of his frustrations and moody outbursts. Our family held lots of tension between my parents and that kept us away from the larger family and the neighbours.

**It was my belief that I wasn't good enough.** I was even useless at cricket and soccer, and that kept me with a low opinion of myself. I longed for my Dad to say, 'Good shot mate' or 'You're OK', with a kind pat on the back. My mother needed to work to help keep the home fires burning and **even this made me feel guilty because of the cost I was to the family.**

**I was a bed-wetter and I remember my first school camp as torture.** I tried to stay awake all night to avoid the embarrassment and horror of another wet bed.

I faked sickness to get out of sitting an entrance test for a position in a private school. The thought of failure or 'I'm not good enough' had me consumed and ashamed of myself.

**One day, I uncovered Dad's pornography and I thought all my birthdays had come at once.** At the time this felt like I had finally connected with my father. Stealing some of his alcohol also made me feel connected to him. Crazy hey? I rapidly became addicted to masturbating and started to look at girls in a different way. I was consumed by lust.

High school was still unkind to me because I couldn't fit in and so I pursued my sexual addiction as my comfort.

My mother and father eventually separated because of Dad's drinking. **As I watched him leave I felt an absolute failure at not being able to stand up to him and fight but instead, to cower and run away.**

I kept taking every opportunity with my lustful thoughts towards girls. The porn was my secret comfort – but I was sadly becoming numb to reality.

My father remarried and as I was coming up to my 21st birthday, I tried to reconnect with him, hoping to start a relationship with him that I'd missed out on as a boy. Soon after, he died in tragic circumstances. Once again I thought it was to do with me and I took it as yet another failure.

I idled along working in a video shop and this only further fed my porn addiction. I deeply regret introducing and pushing lustful videos into the hands of others. I also engaged the services of prostitutes as part of my addictive life. I continued to feel inferior throughout my relationship with the mother of my children and experienced severe bouts of depression.

My work gave me some sense of worth until the section in which I worked was closed down. I saw the replacement job I was given as a 'nothing job'.

## Mark's turning point

My old girlfriend, Mandy, came knocking on my front door to talk to me about her problems. **My partner and children were out so, primed in lust, I set about to fix her problem. Little did I know that she had also become riddled with lust and had done some escort/prostitute work.**

I found this out the hard way!

That day became the beginning of more darkness when my testicles swelled up and I needed medical attention. I had to own up to my partner about all my lies, shame and guilt. **There was no hiding place. My infidelity and shame had come out in the open. I was absolutely helpless when the mother of my children cried and moaned with disgust, torture and woundedness.**

My partner didn't deserve this. She wasn't guilty. But she had to front up with me to the STI clinic for testing. What shame and disgust I had inflicted on her. Fortunately her tests were clear. But that was the straw that broke the camel's back. I went away on a job and on my return the locks on my home had been changed. It was all over Red Rover!

**I became a 'prisoner of male shame' with the penalty written over my cell: 'Never to be released'.** Sad, sad, sad!

Looking back, I wish I'd never let Mandy in the door. I got sucked in like an idiot.

Are you, or do you know a Mark or a Mandy? Riddled with lust? **It's the choices you make not the chances you take that determine your destiny.**

## Mark's healing

I didn't know much about my spirit. I'd had a bit of Sunday School in my younger days but that was it. **But when I met the Creator of the universe for the first time – on a first-name basis – I opened my broken heart to him.** A patch-up job with a bandage couldn't fix this. **God was offering me the way for true deep healing so I chose his way.**

I continue to receive ongoing spiritual healing from God, and the shame pictures are being replaced with his gems from the *Work Manual*. I'm also supported with love and acceptance from my Shed mates and their women. **I take every opportunity to help others who think that recovery is impossible. 'With God all things are possible' (Mark 10:27)."**

---

## Adam and Eve's story

I reckon most of us have heard about Adam and Eve in the Garden of Eden with the 'apple' that caused the stuff-up between them and God.

**The *Work Manual for the Champion Life* (Bible) starts off** with Adam and Eve in the Garden of Eden, living the champion life. The only prohibition was, 'Don't eat the fruit from the tree in the middle of the garden'.

**They eat the fruit and go straight into shame. Adam and Eve blew it big time** and realised they had disobeyed

God so they tried to hide from him. When God went looking for them for their usual afternoon time in the cool of the day he called out, 'Where are you?'

Adam answered, 'I heard you in the garden, and I was afraid because I was naked, so I hid.' No longer free to get around naked, they were ashamed and alienated from the one who had created them.

> **And that's where shame started way back.**
> **It's come right down through time**
> **to hurt all men and women.**
> **That's why I needed to do**
> **the spiritual healing with God**
> **so that I could kick it forever.**

I've got the freedom deep inside. God's promises in the *Work Manual* about shame have worked for me and plenty of other blokes all around the country. That's why we are keen to get our message out.

# 7. Fathers are so important

Morro is one of my treasured younger Shed mates who grew up in a big farming area in Western Australia. He's now in his 40s and a mighty husband and father of 4 children.

After one of my Shed Night trips to the West, he got to do some thinking and talking to God about my shame story. God showed him that even though Morro appears on the surface as a highly successful, confident young leader in his community, deep down he still carried the pain of shame – 'you're not good enough'.

> He hadn't realised that he still believed this lie
> deep,
> deep
> down within.

## A song about shame

We were doing a road trip down south of Perth to another Shed. Morro told me how God had shown him the night before about the lie that he had believed, that had given him shame.

As we drove, on the radio came the Johnny Cash song *A Boy Named Sue*. Wow! What a shame story in that song. We turned up the volume and listened hard to the words.

I've always been a **Johnny Cash** fan. Of his many famous songs this one is worth a closer listen and look by all fathers and sons. **It's a classic shame story that spells out a lot of things we blokes can relate to along the journey of life.**

Have you ever heard *A Boy Named Sue*? It tells the story of a boy whose father walked out when he was just a junior burger. But before he left, he named his son 'Sue' – **and the boy grew up shamed by his name.**

Everyone laughed at Sue, and he went inwards to shame. **He covered it up by being aggressive and angry** – a bit like I did with those poor full-forwards back in my footy days!

Sue travelled around trying to find his father so he could kill him for giving him that terrible name. Finally one day he found him. The two men had a big punch-up, and then drew their guns.

**And that's when his Dad told Sue he gave him that name so he'd grow up tough, because he knew he wouldn't be there to protect his boy.**

> The next thing you know,
> Sue is trying not to cry,
> and calling him his Dad.
> He sees his father differently,
> and his shame is healed.

The song shows the pain we can live in trying to do normal life. It also shows how someone close can cast us into shame and how it can affect our whole purpose.

> Then how freeing
> when someone so close and special
>     can lift us out of shame
>     with an affirming
>     and empowering
>     turbocharged word.
>
> Sue came away with
> a different way of looking at his father and his life.

At the end of the battle of revenge, Sue threw down his weapons and his life changed. He went through his whole life to that point in angry shame fighting for survival. **But a father's acceptance and being able to bring the pain out into the light and most of all hearing an affirming word from his Pa, released the pain of the shame** of his girl's name. He saw things differently.

## Morro's story

Morro's father wasn't anything like Sue's Dad, and his story is very different to that song. But his shame came from misunderstanding something his Dad did to protect him!

**When he was 12, Morro thought he was the only farm boy in his district who wasn't allowed to drive a tractor by himself.** His Dad never told him why and he never asked.

**Morro thought there must have been something wrong with him.** Morro has always had a good relationship with his Dad – **it was just a case of a boy not asking his Dad.** See how innocence can cause wrong thinking? In time, after watching his neighbours' younger sisters driving the tractor, Morro's self-doubt took hold.

Without his Dad knowing, he did get to drive a tractor on another property. This helped him to be accepted by his other 12-year-old tractor-driving mates. But this shame lie still haunted Morro deep down, even though he hadn't realised it was affecting him until he heard my story. That prompted him to go straight to the top to ask God for guidance.

> See how subtle this can be –
> this cheat called shame?
> So watch out for those little monsters.

God showed Morro another 'killing' moment when he was a 17-year-old mechanic.

One day Morro's boss was in a heated conversation with a big customer over a job disagreement. Morrow, still fairly shy and introverted, was standing beside his boss minding his own business.

Next minute the angry customer turned on Morro and gave him a blast. 'What are you standing here listening to our conversation for? I'm not paying you to stand around doing nothing. Get that broom and start sweeping.'

Morro went into horror shock and again went inward for his defence – 'I'm not good enough, I'm not good enough.'

## Morro's healing

Now if you know the Morro of today you'd know of his pretty successful public life in radio announcing, public speaking, songwriting and singing. He's also the chaplain of the West Coast Eagles. Morro wrote a song *Heal Our Land,* which he sang at Angus Buchan's South African property in front of 300,000 men. No-one would have believed that until recently he had carried self-doubt.

> **The Good News is that Morro is free.**
> **He recognised the lie**
> **and what it had done to him,**
> **    and gave it to God.**
> **He's accepted**
> **God's promises of spiritual healing**
> **    from the inside out.**

## What can we learn?

Firstly, as parents, **let's ensure our children are encouraged to always feel free to ask, 'Why?'** – even when we're doing something for their own good. And let's make time to answer their 'why' questions.

Secondly, **we need to deal with the little things – like a childhood misunderstanding – that might cause us shame without us realising it,** and hang on to us for years. Don't take them aboard. Let them go through to the Keeper.

What if Morro didn't go for the spiritual freedom?

Do you think drugs would have been the way to give him confidence? Under the right medical supervision, prescription medication can help people who need it. However, I'm really talking about the chronic use of recreational drugs. It might seem like a quick fix, but it's just a cover-up with long-term painful results.

I reckon the escalating usage of recreational drugs doesn't show good results or fix the problem. It's a short-term cover-up with long-term problems. **Men's mental health is one of our greatest challenges. I think that until we are able to help men be comfortable in their hearts, spirits and souls the problem will continue.**

If you're not the real you because shame holds you back with fear, your creativity and innovation won't happen. **There are parts of you that don't get to come out**. They can be smashed on the inside.

The best is yet to come from you. Let it come out!

**You're never too old to learn or change, but you've just gotta wanna.**

Maybe we fathers have a need to apologise to our sons for something a bit like the Johnny Cash song. Have we been 'calling our boys Sue'? We might have shamed them with a smart remark or called them a killing name that had the same effect as calling them 'Sue'.

**The boy named Sue searched all his life and nearly killed himself chasing revenge** – but all he wanted was his Dad to acknowledge him and explain why he had that name. Then his attitude changed. If he forgave his Dad – wow, freedom.

> **The ones closest to us
> – our parents or our children –
> are usually the ones who hurt us the most.
> Take care.**

If the words of this old song spoke to you take heart, you now have the tools to fix the problem. **Give up the right to get even with those who hurt you because that takes too much of your heart and head and it hurts. You've gotta wanna give it up.**

> **A gem from the *Work Manual***
>
> Forgive us our sins as we also forgive everyone who sins against us. (Luke 11:4 NIV)

### Watto's way to pray

Dear God,
Please help me to know the killing moment of my shame. Help me to forgive the person/s who put the lie on my soul. Thank you for my new heart, spirit and mind so I can live on with freedom. Thank you in Jesus' name.

# 8. Striking the gold, kicking shame

Whether you believed a lie of worthlessness as a very young fella or whether you got a raw deal as an adult, you can deal with it. You can win the battle over shame and learn how to keep your guard up for possible future telltale signs – and how not to take shame on again. Also, you can stop and think when you're about to say or do something that may push a person into the prison of male shame.

**You've gotta know when to hold 'em, when to fold 'em, and when to walk away.**

I've said it before and I'll say it again **'I've never seen a bloke (or woman) go backwards with encouragement'.** So be encouraged. I needed to make this a spiritual choice to be free of the 50 years of shame that thought it had me by the long and shorts.

**You'll never never know till you hava hava go!**

## What Jesus did with shame

Jesus died to actually take the shame of man away and free us. He took the shame and threw it into the pits of hell, never to come back to that person.

> **A gem from the *Work Manual***
>
> …by cancelling the record of debt that stood against us with its legal demands. This [Jesus] set aside, nailing it to the cross. He disarmed the rulers and authorities and put them to open shame, by triumphing over them in him. (Colossians 2:14–15 ESV)

Back in those times when Jesus died on the cross, after they'd fought their battles, they would bring the prisoners of war back and chain them up and walk them through the city. They had to pay the price of being defeated, and they were put in the prison or locked up.

> When we're in shame,
> we feel like
> we're the one being paraded through the town,
> > but
> > in actual fact,
> Jesus is taking our shame
> and parading it through the town
> > – not us.

We might feel like we're being dragged through the streets because we've been shamed and made a laughing stock of. That might be how we feel inside.

But he actually died to take that away from us, take the shame through the streets, and ping it to the pits of hell. **That's how he feels about your shame, not about you.**

So, all those voices that want to accuse us, saying 'you're worthless' – we shouldn't let them in. They are powerless because of Jesus.

If Jesus the Champion of champion blokes died on the cross to take all of our shame, why not give him a go? **Give your shame to him and don't take it back.** He will exchange your shame for freedom. That's what the cross is all about.

He gave 100% on the cross – so why give him less than 100% in letting go of this muck called shame. **How can we expect 100% healing if we're not prepared to let 100% go for freedom?** Come on, you can do it!

If we don't accept God's promise and get on with it, it's a tough battle on our own. Do we think we're better than Jesus and we don't need him? – Huh! If we ditch this, then where do we turn? It's like the boy pushing the loaded barrow up the hill. He's got the job ahead of him.

**Could the reason we have such a record of failure in relationships in the world today be that we're not doing it his way to smash shame?** Get clear and clean to start again! Don't take all the pain and shame of the past into a new relationship.

It's a tough battle if we try to do it on our own – like the boy pushing a loaded barrow up a hill.

### A gem from the *Work Manual*

Confess your sins to each other and pray for each other so that you may be healed. (James 5:16 NIV)

> **Watto's version of James 5:16**
>
> Spill ya guts. Get rid of the muck (shame)
> so you can become the real-deal
> champion you were created to be.

## Keep it simple

Don't forget the old KISS principle – 'keep it simple stupid' and get on with it.

**It may take you some courage to let your creativity, your passion, emotions and dreams come out, but if you let fear of ridicule or rejection win, chances are that you'll continue holding back.**

Years ago I heard this, and I've discovered it's true:

> Every time you come up with a new idea,
> you'll have to go through
> >ridicule and rejection
> to get to acceptance.
> It's a natural thing.
> It's gonna happen.
> It doesn't mean it's not a good idea.
> Don't be put off by it.
> So have courage to tough it out
> >through the first two Rs.

Let it flow! It's so exciting to see a bloke coming alive.

When growing up were you an 'ideas' bloke who liked to make things happen in one way or another? Your ideas, dreams, initiatives and creativity might have been encouraged, watered and nurtured – or were they mostly ridiculed when you put a new one forward? Were your ideas when at school squashed, ridiculed or made fun of? If so, it would have been easier for you to put your head down, shut up shop and put your creativity to sleep.

**We can plod along in the same old, same old boring zone where nothing changes because nothing changes.** We never get to know what it could be like – thinking, 'If only!' or 'I shoulda!'

It's so important to have the freedom to grow up being the real you. **If you weren't allowed to be yourself growing up, it's OK. Start now.** And maybe you can help children around you – your own or other people's – have the freedom to be themselves.

Do you still want to make things happen? When you're in shame, with your head down and not feeling good, the music just doesn't come out of you. Society says, 'Never give a sucker a break.'

> **But there's opportunities in Australia all the time, and even people who are looked upon as**
> > **suckers**
> > **or down-and-outers**

> can grab them,
> once they're free to be the real deal
> > and secure in who they are.
> > > Shed your shame and grab those opportunities.

If you're OK and you're secure in who you are, be ready, because the sucker can get that break. You can go for it. It's powerful.

**Back yourself in and you'll soon know that it's not real hard when you're havin' a go.**

### Shame hates the light

Can you see how shame can breed fear in families, teams, workplaces, churches, political parties – in any culture? It can act like termites. **The shame word is not much different to the sh*t word. They both need to be dumped.**

Shame is disconnection, isolation, feeling unloved and worthless.

**Shame hates exposure, heaps of love, connection and a feeling of belonging.** We blokes want to love and be loved – we want to connect and most of all we want to belong. We want to feel relevant. So take this aboard 'cause these things become the greatest healers of shame. **Winners are grinners.**

## Col's story

Col is one of my treasured Shed mates. He wishes to tell a part of his shame story to help others into freedom.

Col and I were in the same class at high school, so our mateship goes over 50 years. We met up again recently and Col bought my first book and felt that he would like to attend the monthly Shed meetings at my truckyard.

**Col firmly believes that our actual meeting was not by chance but due to a purpose from the Big Fella upstairs.** We now do a great part of our spiritual life together at Shed Happens. We are in each other's Sheds. We can be counted on.

## Col's shame story

Most would say this champion mate was dealt a throwaway card from the pack at the start of the game of his life through none of his own doings.

Col was always quiet. He had a much darker complexion than everyone else in our class – his lovely skin made me look very pale. Unbeknown to me, Col's inside **battle was about his true identity because he had a very different complexion from the rest of his family. His question was: 'Where do I fit in here?'**

Not one of his relatives was allowed to reveal to him anything about who he was, so Col's journey through school was tough and sometimes cruel. It was always about the colour of his skin, with many poisonous words that kept driving him deep into himself. He came to believe that he was no good.

His unhappy family home caused him more shame. As he walked to school the day after a loud argument by his parents the previous night, he felt that everyone in the street was peering through the curtains to see him as the kid living in the house where all the fighting came from.

**This growing lie caused him to dream and wish he was a black snake so he could slide out of the house,** under the gate, and into the gutter to get to school without being seen by anyone. And that's how low he came to feel because he was carrying all the guilt and shame for something he was not responsible for.

For many years of his life Col struggled with never being told he was loved and dealing with feelings of isolation and worthlessness.

**None of us has any say in who our parents are.** You've just gotta cop it – that's our dealt card.

## Col's family secret

His family was sworn to cover the shame that Col was carrying because back then, that's just how it was. But one day Col's brother told him that he was the result of his mother's affair with someone from a South American background.

Col grew up and married. When one of Col's sons was born, the doctors couldn't work out what was causing bruising on his bottom.

Two years later, their little boy needed to visit a doctor who happened to be an American. He quickly identified **the bruising that hadn't gone away since birth as a 'blue spot', a type of birthmark unique to people of certain races.** This caused Col to be severely challenged again by fact that his skin colour had its origins in adultery.

## Col's healing

In his 30s, Col eventually called out to the Creator of the universe for answers. He asked his Heavenly Father to show him who he really was. The answers started coming through a wonderful caring preacher friend and at last some light started to flicker.

Col continues his healing journey from shame. He takes in the spiritual promises from the *Work Manual*.

> The shame that was like a huge boil
>    has burst
>    and been cleaned out of all the pus.
>    The new skin is regrowing.
> Col knows his true worth
> and the hole is being quickly filled in with love.

Col knows that Jesus took his shame once and for all at the cross and he chooses not to go back to the old place. Nowadays he is pleased to share his story, not to belittle his parents, but to encourage others who might be carrying undeserved shame – so they can see that there is hope for a brighter future.

Col and his wife now have children and grandchildren. His encouragement to them today is of loving forgiveness and of constantly declaring freedom from any part of his battle that they may have taken aboard during their lives.

Col is a mighty living example of freedom. He is able to help and encourage many others in similar battles of shame.

**He's come from the sewer of shame – the grease trap of the soul – to freedom of the soul forever.**

---

### Another gem from the *Work Manual*

Do not be afraid. **You will not suffer shame.** Do not fear disgrace; you will not be humiliated. **You will forget the shame of your youth**… (Isaiah 54:4 NIV)

# 9. Your choice

**Fellas it's your choice. You decide what you want. Shame? Or success – spiritual freedom? Your choice – stop your stinkin' thinking. You may need to change your mind more than your behaviour.**

Get rid of the viruses in your internal computer. Replace the chip. Ask the Creator of the universe to do an inside job without stitches.

We can believe that we're so bad – or so something else – that even God can't forgive us.

### The truth about how the Big Fella sees our shame

Stop bashing your heart.

**Let go and let the Big Fella**.

Spiritually we can dump our shame and our failings at the cross where Jesus was nailed. No beating around the bush. This is the promise from the *Work Manual*. It's your call!

**Choose love.**

Our hearts were made for love, connection and belonging and worth.

**Shame hates love.**

> Shame kills these beautiful qualities,
> so keep your wits about you.
> Our heart is where it all starts.
>
> The heart of the problem
> is the problem of the heart.

Mate, how do you go when someone close gets a little too close to the raw part of you? Do you batten down the hatches or do a runner so you don't have to expose the lie that you aren't good enough?

The heart of the problem is the problem of the heart!

Do you have your guard up at all times? **The more we cover it the more it hurts us on the inside.**

---

**Watto's version of the *Work Manual* in 1 John 3:19-21**

When you battle in your own strength you bash your heart too much. But when you come to know that God knows our hearts and all that goes on inside it and that he's bigger than ours, then we can 'get it' and let him in on the battle.

---

We don't have to put up with the lie anymore. It's our choice.

If we say we don't need God and his spiritual healing, how come there are so many people living under shame? When will we realise we can't fix it in our own strength? Plenty try, try, try, and it's hard not to go back to the hole.

## Healing with or without the Big Fella

Fellas, I've tried to give you a big look at this monster so we can now see where it may be weaselling away at us, eating us inside.

The way society directs us to get some healing from shame without the Big Fella works to a degree and I encourage that – it all helps and is good. We're better off already, but if you can look realistically at the spiritual part of who you are, it can take you to the total freedom.

> It sure worked for me
> and I hope you can get it also.
> You're safe –
>     I didn't get a squeaky voice.
>     It's not wussy –
> it's so freeing
> and you can appreciate others who also battle.
> You are able to show
>     more tolerance and patience to them,
> helping them become real-deal champions too.

Champions, healing is on the inside in our heart and soul. Learn to forgive bit-by-bit, step-by-step. This can be pretty hard in so many situations. **Ask for forgiveness where you've inflicted shame onto someone. If you do this alone you're going to need courage – like never before and lots of it.**

*The Big Fella will give you the spiritual strength to let it go!*

But if you choose to go to the spiritual part of you, you don't do forgiveness on your own from your head. The Big Fella will give you the spiritual strength to let it go.

We more than likely will need to ask forgiveness too for our attitudes and actions towards those who have treated us badly and caused us to suffer for what might have been many years. There's also the people we may have shamed, and we need to get it right.

**Fellas, this is the way I would have this chat with God.** And sometimes it's good to just speak this out aloud.

### Watto's way to pray about this

Dear God,
Please help me with courage to forgive the person/s or organisation or things that put me down into the 'prison of male shame'. Would you please fix my heart so that it beats in time with yours? In Jesus' name. Thank you very much. Amen.

Another story from a Shed mate, but first something about telling stories.

## You can't argue with a man's story

One of my lifetime mates of over 50 years just so happens to totally disagree with my politics and my footy team. Our friendship and mateship is far too important to carry on like pork chops and go beyond the point of offending each other. But **it's so healthy for us to hear each other's views on all topics. It makes us grow up. We might not change each other's minds,** but we see the bigger picture and are less judgemental.

The unwritten law seems to be no talkie about politics, sex, religion!

How about this?

> You can argue with a man
>     about his political views,
>     his choice of football team,
>     his religious belief,
> but
> you can't argue with his story.

His story is his story. **So the more we hear a bloke's shame story the more we see it smashed.**

**The unwritten law growing up in our country seems to be no talkie about politics, sex and religion.** I reckon this holds us back. We learn so much from listening to each other and we miss out on this wisdom.

**'Silence is golden', but sometimes silence can be yellow. We hide behind it, wimping out.**

Another person's viewpoint doesn't need to hurt us. It gives us the bigger picture of life seen through another pair of eyes.

So what's gone wrong? Let's sort it out.

These two champion Shed blokes found their 'moment' of shame in physical conditions they had no control over. Check it out.

## Owen's story

One year at a men's conference, God prompted me to speak to 190 blokes on what he had taught me about shame. I finished by saying that **I would be available after dinner for a bit of a Shed shame chat for anyone who wanted to take a deeper look at this topic**.

Eighty of those 190 blokes turned up! I asked for a show of hands if anyone had a specific moment of shame that God had shown them as a result of my session talk. It might be something they'd never, ever discussed. Eight blokes raised their hand. I got each of them to have a one-on-one chat with one of my experienced Shed interviewers. Then each man had 10 minutes to talk to the whole group from the deepest part of his heart about his shame.

> **One after the other,
> men realised they were in a
>     safe non-judgemental place.
> They were able to talk publicly
> for the first time
> about the hidden poison and its consequences
> that had spilled all over
>     those who were close and loved by them.**

**The healing of their shame began for those men and others as they opened up at this mighty weekend.**

The next morning Owen limped to the brekkie table and I said, 'What's wrong mate?'

He replied, 'I've broken my foot'.

'What? Where's your plaster?'

He then pulled up the leg of his tracky dacks and showed me his wooden leg and foot – and yes, the foot part had split across the middle.

## Owen's shame 'moment'

**Owen had covered up his wooden leg for years** but now he was given a moment of grace by God. He told me what happened to him as a 12-year-old fun-loving and sports-crazy boy helping his Dad on the farm.

His Dad was on the tractor about to dig a hole with the auger. Owen was standing holding the marker and out of nowhere he was caught in the underground netting and dragged into the hole. All in one horrible moment he had his leg ripped off. Terrible, terrible accident. Whose fault? No-one knows.

**As a sad result, in the past 40 years his Dad in his shame has never ever said a word to Owen about the incident.** He left it up to Owen's Mum to do the talking.

Owen felt like he was the guilty one and so took his fate into shame. Because of his wooden leg, Owen lost his self-confidence at school, in sport and later with girls. He went inwards, never speaking a word about the tragic mishap that had spiralled a father and a son into guilt and shame for so long.

**Owen had been able to cover his wooden leg without a limp** but after he broke his foot it opened the whole story of his boyhood shame. It also allowed one of the other blokes at the weekend to get the grinder out and with a few screws and a little plating to have Owen's foot all patched up.

## Owen's healing

That night he sat out front of the entire crowd of blokes, pulled up his trouser leg and said, '**No more do I carry this lie of shame that I'm no good. Forty years of pain gone! Thank you to the Big Fella for sorting me out.**'

Owen didn't instantly lose what he had held inside for 40 years. It was hard for him to let go and he needed spiritual healing.

> **He had to learn to choose
> and to take authority
> not to go back there to his hidden place of pain,
> which was his usual defensive reaction.**

But once Owen got this sorted out he could go see his old Dad and speak forgiveness and make peace with him. Now both have healed hearts.

There ain't one bit of shame that can't be destroyed!

If Owen and his Dad knew way back then what they know today, how much pain could have been avoided? It's so important to get stuff sorted out as soon as possible and get on with freedom. **You've just gotta wanna. You're never too old to learn or change.** Just do it!

## Let's shed our shame

This is a guarantee for you: There ain't one bit of shame that can't be destroyed.

> **A gem from the *Work Manual***
> Unto you, O Lord, do I bring my life. O my God, I trust, lean on, rely on, and am confident in you. Let me not be put to shame or (my hope in you) be disappointed; let not my enemies triumph over me. (Psalm 25:1 Amp)

If we're like Owen, we get to know that when we refuse the lie about our wooden leg or our one arm or our bald head, there's more. **It's who we are, not what we look like that matters.**

As we roll on in life through school and into the workplace there are countless other things that can take away our self-worth and try to shame us.

**We cop verbal shame through subtle supposed 'jokes'** – killing, hurtful words about our bodies, size and shape or colour, the way we speak. **They can come not only from our parents or friends, but others too**, and we can feel hopeless, different and ugly in various forms of bullying. They all can kill us on the inside.

How are you going with this chapter? Hang in there – you're on a winner.

**This is an old saying but it's more wrong than right: 'Sticks and stones will break my bones but names will never hurt me!'**

> More often than not,
> names and bullying can and do
> cripple us into shame
>    if we hear them enough.
> At what point do we weaken and believe it?

Many of us have been hurt big time as kids. The name-calling stays with us and bites us all through our lives. You know what I mean?

## Vic's story

Vic was born a very unwell little boy. He had a serious condition, and needed lots of care. One of the nurses was his life-saving angel. His first 9 months required Vic to have special treatment because his little hands were literally stuck together. They had to be prised apart and bathed and massaged. His armpits, wrists and knees required constant attention to free his movements.

Vic attended primary school, but with a speech impediment he couldn't put words together. He also had dyslexia. **He had high and special needs, and withdrew into himself. Vic chose not to try to talk to anyone.** He spent more school time outside with the groundsman working on the oval. And because he couldn't put words together, he shut up!

High school was worse. **Vic was bullied about not being able to read or write so he shut down more and went inwards.** Anger was his revenge – belting and yelling at those who drove him into shame. Some students called him dumbo and an idiot. Vic believed he was hopeless because of not being able to read or write.

## Vic's healing

**His mother was his saving grace.** One day he went with Mum and her friend to a church. On the way, the lady told Vic that **Jesus loved him, that he was special to him and that he had a plan for him in his future life.**

> Vic heard this in his heart
> and the seed of worth began to grow in him.

Vic left school at 13 and missed out on his teenage years by working like a man and being with men all day. He found that his gift was to work with his hands. He could build anything and fix machinery. He was a jack-of-all-trades.

So from believing the lie that he was a dummy going through school he started to find he had worth with his hands. Vic met a young lady – and there was love in the air. **Their journey of love began and still burns brightly to this day.**

They travelled around Australia together hoping to find a dream for their future. Vic used those hands-on skills to do his talking. Then they were given an opportunity (all expenses paid) to attend Bible School and things looked great. Vic's wife wrote all the assignments while Vic listened and watched.

After having to do a video presentation in front of the class Vic began to feel his worthlessness again. **The lie that he was dumb was reignited when the teacher told him that he wouldn't be able to make it in ministry.**

So back into the shame lie he was driven. However **God's plan and hope for Vic resurfaced.**

Vic knew his freedom from his shame after seeing the birth of his children, feeling real-deal worth. He believes God's promise of healing from Jesus who took away his shame at the cross.

Vic's hands-on ministry today continues to help many, many young people through the pain and hurts of their past. He is able to encourage them to get to know God on a first-name basis and trust in his promise. He has God's love in his heart and passes it on.

## It's winnable!

> I've said it before,
> but I'm saying it again:
> > shame hates love,
> > > light
> > > and positive empowering words
> > > spoken over it.
> It hates being exposed.

**It needs to be brought out from hiding under the carpet and exposed to the brightness** of a golden life for you.

It's winnable. You need a safe place and a trusted person where you can get it out.

# 10. Grace

Champions, back to the Big Fella's grace – this one can take a lot of getting used to. Society says you must 'do' and you have to 'pay' – no such thing as a free feed.

**Well, God's way is totally different. Fellas, you just have to receive for free his healing stuff and it's called grace.** Sometimes your life might look really ugly and that's the place you may be in before you ask for his help. But out of ugly, that's where you'll meet grace. **Grace is more than a girl's name!**

Grace is more than a girl's name!

### Getting out of pain and ugliness

> When you're in deep pain with shame
>     it is ugly –
> but then Jesus,
> the bloke who got dirty feet,
> comes along and starts doing his teaching
> and 'loving his brother'
> before being nailed to the cross.
>
> He turned the ugly place we're in
> into his beautiful grace for every one of us.

You may have started off fragile in your ugly place, but once you are willing to sort it out and become a little more vulnerable, it becomes easier.

**If you've been doing life only by society's way it can be hard to open up to believe and receive that this grace is free from the Creator of the universe.** It can be a challenge to accept it.

Why are so many of us walking around everywhere in the deep pain of shame – even in and out of the churches? Why, why, why? **That's the whole guts of why the Champion Jesus went to the cross to take it upon himself. Let's stop pussyfooting around.**

Make choices or take chances?

It's up to us.

## How to recognise shame

**Have another bo-peep at these telltale things to consider.**

- A shamed person can be **so controlling and so rigid** that it drives everyone crazy. You just want to switch off in their company or steer way clear of them.
- **A shamed person tries to be perfect** to kill the inner pain. They try to get attention with 'look at me, look at me, look how good I am, see how well I do things?' The perfectionist just likes to do things right all the time (his way). He's constantly bashing himself trying all the time

to overachieve and win approval to try to get some of the love he missed out on.

- A shamed person can **live and act numb** – just to avoid more pain.

- A shamed person can have **difficulty with intimate relationships** especially in the sexual part because they feel so low about themselves. They can be too embarrassed to try.

- A shamed person **frequently blames others** to divert attention from himself to keep his ego intact and avoid answering hard questions.

- A shamed person may **overpower others with judgemental comments**. He might try to shame others to keep them at bay to make himself feel superior (as I did).

- A shamed person **needs to be right all the time** and continually hammers his point home – a pain in the neck.

## Sort it out!

Fellas, I reckon we've got the picture pretty well about **this poison of shame** by now.

> Sadly
> we can keep sipping slowly,
> not even knowing,
> and then one day gasping for healing

> 'cause the poison is killing us on the inside.
> Well I want to assure you
> that I've seen many, many blokes get the Gold,
>     the freedom.
> They usually get to a point
>     – it's like a 'moment' where they get it –
> and then away they go!

They identify the lie, they look at it and they want to kick it.

**Most blokes want to keep it simple and sort it out. They can 'spill' it to a trusted person or people and pour the bright lights onto it.** Sometimes they might want to get professional help from a counsellor who specialises in shame, so they can get healing and help.

> **Overpower shame with
>     kind,
>     loving,
>     positive words
> and replace the picture of destruction
> with a new and positive picture.
>         Wow!**

Then healed blokes want to help other blokes get it sorted out.

## Healthy shame?

Can there be such a thing as 'healthy shame' if shame is so destroying? Just say you do something on the spur of the moment and make an absolute fool of yourself but quickly come to your senses and say, 'No way is this scummy shame going be part of me'.

**You copped the instant wake-up call and took it as a challenge to deal with straight away. No more of that! We could call that healthy shame.**

## Let's stop shaming our women!

**Fellas, the main things that shame a female are about her looks and her body shape, and whether she fits in with the group. 'Am I OK?'**

If you have a woman to love and she loves you, or even if you don't have one, you'll want to know this Gold for your future. Have a think about these things that hurt and can shame her the most.

**She needs to feel appreciated, not worthless.**

> So with any smart wisecracks,
> thinking we're being funny
> at her expense,
> forget it.

Let's cut it out because no-one wins.

Margaret tells me that when women are trying to buy clothes, it can be painful when looking at themselves with all the mirrors and bright lights. They just don't look as good as they'd like to and they focus on all that's wrong with their bodies.

I'm repeating this because we blokes need to get it big time. Her body image and shape are usually the major thing for her. Not feeling cool with the pretty girl group around her can also have her shamed into non-belonging.

It's unfair to expose women to the things they want to hide – they may like privacy. Some women can feel like they are fat, stupid or ugly – how that thinking cripples them and keeps them from having healthy and loving relationships!

**This also affects young girls 'cause school can be so cruel when they cop shaming words from the boys or adult males in their lives.**

**Fellas, no harm to women or children.** We must cut out the smart comments about their body bits and shapes. We best encourage them with loving comments and then you'll see Gold come your way.

## Two ways to shed shame

Champions, what can we do to control the shame monster, or more importantly to completely take him out? No more shame, no more pain – your choice. Yes it's your choice.

**You have to decide if you want healing and also decide if you want the world's way of healing without the Big Fella's help, or the extra turbocharged healing in your spirit and soul.** If you want to stick to the world's way, that's OK and good – I just want you to know that there's also more available.

> Let's be well aware of the fact
> that shame doesn't want to be spoken out about.
> It has its way of keeping in our deep dark place
> and practically gagging us –
> that's what makes it thrive.

**So the most important thing we can do is publicly expose our shame.**

Make a choice – you have that freedom.

Shame or freedom.

More exposure = more freedom.

It's up to you – you can do it!

If you choose to deny the spiritual part of who you are in this area, that's your call and it's OK by me. **That won't stop us tackling it head on for as much freedom as possible.**

So don't let shame gag you – especially if you are a perfectionist 'cause you won't want to be seen as having anything wrong with you.

## The world's way, without the Big Fella's help

The way to be free from the shame prison without the Big Fella looks like this:

- **Make a choice** not to believe the lie about yourself.
- **Speak to a trusted person** and get it out of your head. The more vulnerable you are, the more healing will come. So let it come out.
- **Avoid isolation** – it can get too dark and too lonely too quickly on your own.
- If you need help, **book a time with a professional counsellor** who works in the shame area.
- **Know the difference between guilt and shame**.
- **Replace negative thinking with positive**.
- If you feel shame – or identify any shame telltale signs of worthlessness – don't stress. **Take note and act as soon as possible.** Tell it where to go, don't take it aboard.

## The spiritual way, with the Big Fella's help

The Big Fella's spiritual way to be free from the shame prison:

- **All of the above. All of that stuff is good, but there can be more…**
- **Connect with some other blokes who know the Creator of the universe** for support and encouragement.
- Talk to the Champion of champions – that's **prayer**.
- **Forgive and be forgiven.**
- **Replace your stinkin' thinking with gems from the Work Manual.**
- If you are a member of a church or Christian group, **accept healing** when you have a meal with Jesus (taking the bread and wine which is called Holy Communion).

And don't forget to shoot up a 'thank you God' prayer along the way in your freedom.

Christian spiritual healing can be encouraged by a like-minded community with love and appropriate touch and prayer, but that's your choice. It's not for me to push or preach. It's my call to encourage and love my brothers and lots of times **I only use words where absolutely necessary. Don't tell 'em, show 'em.**

## My choice

After a lot of blood, sweat and tears and years of growing up **I chose to accept the spiritual part of who I am.** I chose to know whose I am. I chose to have the Big Fella's help. I needed the works to sort out my shame.

Shame thought it had me – but no way. I got you in the end, shame, and I'm not going back to that place ever again!

So if you are at this challenging place of being not sure and wondering whether God is the real deal, this is how I did it.

**I called out to God one day and asked him if he was for real.** I asked him, if he was real, could he show me in my life and nobody else's that he was for real. Otherwise this 'God bit' was all a fairytale.

So I just kept asking him to show me more.

That's how it happened for me. I certainly didn't tell anyone that I was having a serious chat to him and at the end of the day it really got down to just the two of us. So don't get diverted – go straight to the top.

**I got a heart job by the Big Fella from the inside out without stitches.** I spoke about it earlier in this book and in Chapter 12 of *Every Bloke's a Champion – Even You!* Since then, I have Margaret and a close group of blokes who make Shed

Happens happen for me. We talk out anything that I need help with.

**Shed it! Shed it! Shed it! Speak it out – get it? And be healed and free.**

I wish someone could have gotten through to me way back. I was caught up in the problems I saw in 'religious' things and people, and I got lost in the Stuff.

I needed to know that all I had to do was to go straight to the top – to God, the Big Fella, the Creator of the universe.

**So if we say we know and follow the Big Fella – how come we just don't accept his freedom over shame? We can sit in church week after week and keep the door of our heart shut.** So if this is you, maybe it's time to have a red-hot talk to him. Say you're sorry and accept his promise and you'll get out of the prison of male shame.

## Points to remember

- Once you see your moment of shame, don't be scared of it. Think: OK, how do I get rid of this? **It's like dropping off ten bags of cement off your shoulders.** But speak out with courage – admit it and get ready for the battle. This muck hurts, it's disappointing and it can be almost crippling. It's like your computer chip is jammed and you

## How good is this?

So the more I asked God about shame, the more he showed me there was more freedom – enough for every man and woman in the freeing of shame.

And **the more I tell my story the more I hear amazing stories of freedom.** So now, after speaking and seeing many new and exciting free men and women it was time to write this book so more Champions could gain freedom.

No more shame, but freedom to be more the real-deal bloke you were created to be.

Champions, thanks for doing this journey of freedom from shame.

There's no time like the present.

Take the Gold promised.

Use it and pass it on.

Enjoy life.

See you in the Shed.

**And I've never seen a bloke (or a woman) go backwards with encouragement.**

*Keep Amazing Grace!*

*Watto*

# Every Bloke's a Champion... Even You!

> 'I've never seen a bloke go backwards with encouragement.'

Finances, fatherhood, divorce, depression, anger, broken dreams. The modern male has a lot to contend with. But Watto says every bloke's a champion, even you—and he means it. His straightforward words-from-the-heart help men achieve the turbocharged life they've dreamed of but never thought they could have.

**Ian has a wonderful knack for telling it how it is.** Andrew Ireland, CEO Sydney Swans football club

**This book is for you, champ, whoever and wherever you are.**
Phil Smith, ABC Radio 'Weekends with Phil'

**This book is written from real life experience in a language the average punter can understand with stories we can relate to.**
Paul Morrison, Chaplain, West Coast Eagles football club

**Watto will encourage your heart and put a fire in your belly.**
Peter Janetzki, Talking Life, Radio 96five

**The stuff Watto talks about will help set you free... it did for my husband, and in doing so, has revitalised our marriage.**
Julie Oster, Farmer

**Pick up Watto's book, have a read and let change begin.** Timothy Nagel, Airline Pilot

'Champion, I'd love to meet you at Shed Happens!'

**wattobooks.com — shednight.com**

www.ingramcontent.com/pod-product-compliance
Lightning Source LLC
LaVergne TN
LVHW052255070426
835507LV00035B/2908